American Christian

One Body Many Members

SANTANNA LOZANO

WESTBOW PRESS®
A DIVISION OF THOMAS NELSON & ZONDERVAN

WestBow Press books may be ordered through booksellers or by contacting:

WestBow Press
A Division of Thomas Nelson & Zondervan
1663 Liberty Drive
Bloomington, IN 47403
www.westbowpress.com
844-714-3454

ISBN: 978-1-6642-7847-9 (sc)
ISBN: 978-1-6642-7846-2 (e)

Print information available on the last page.

WestBow Press rev. date: 10/17/2022

My testimony Hi, my name is Santanna lozano and I'm an American Christian. My testimony is actually quite long but I'm gonna hit on three points of it, that being the past, my conversion and my present.

My past: I was born in Fredericksburg,TX which is a small tourist town, but I grew up and lived fourteen miles away in a smaller town known as Stonewall. As children we attended the stonewall baptist church and it was at the age of four that one Sunday the pastor told us, that if we asked Jesus to come into our hearts that he would come in and that we would get to be with him. I'm starting here because it was this memory that I remember best. We walked into a room and all of us sat down and the lights were turned off and I prayed a simple prayer asking Jesus to come into my heart.It was right at this moment that my world stepped into a whole new realm of reality. When I got home I remember looking at my parents and not fully understanding what was going on; it was as though I saw them walking but could feel the emptiness inside them, like empty shells of flesh. I wasn't sure what to do, but that wasn't all that happened to me either. I got an understanding that one day I would die and not just me but everyone that I know would one day die. I remember crying and my parents trying their best to comfort me,but I kept insisting that I could die and I refused to take their words of comfort. I personally believe that at that moment after asking Jesus to come into my heart, that the Holy Spirit chose to give me a gift mentioned as the gift of discerning of spirits; we will talk about this possibly later on. This book isn't to argue theology, but I do want to be honest with every single thing that I believe fully that God did with me through me and to me. My life began to get a lot worse as more things became a lot more noticeable and as I got a taste of the three things that Have always enticed humanity. That is the lust of the flesh, the lust of the eyes and the pride of life. Because there is much more I wanna write about I'm going to skip forward to the point right before my conversion. I will hit on some of what I went through later on for the sake of understanding that God can use you the way he is using me. I'm going to leave a list below of some of the stuff I had done from this point to when my conversion happens.

Prideful	Homosexuality	Started getting tattooed at 12yrs old
Anger	Rage	Affiliated with gangs
Depression	Suicidal	Sold drugs
Frustration	Mocking	Having two kids unmarried
Lustful	Calling myself a god	Leaving my pregnant girlfriend and son
Masturbation	Hatred	Got arrested for robbing nine cars and than running from the cops
Pornography	Trying to molest somebody I loved	Fighting
Sex before marriage with multiple people/ fornicator	Drinking to not feel or to cope	
Manipulation	Thoughts of murder	
Controlling	Being a compulsive Liar	
Sex with a married woman	Abusing people	
Dishonoring my mother and father	Abusing animals out of anger	
Drugs	A thief	
Bitterness	Witchcraft/New age	
Lover of self	Joined a cult	
Orphan mentality	Lover of money/greed	
Cheating on everyone	Slanderous	
Unsatisfied	Murdered an animal to see if I can do it	
Cutting myself	Tattooing myself in rebellion	

Therefore I tell you, her sins, which are many, are forgiven—for she loved much. But he who is forgiven little, loves little."- Luke 7:47 (ESV)

(Picking back up now roughy three months before my conversion)

Meeting one of Gods Daughter's I'm around nineteen or twenty years old now and I had left my girlfriend and son. We had been separated about six months and life was getting worse. I was living with a friend at the time and that wasn't going well either; after all I was lost. I had a lot of bad stuff happened to me And I finally was just done. I ended up helping a person get heroin who was also pregnant and after that I didn't know what to do anymore. I walked back inside and thought to myself I should just kill myself. I didn't know what to do anymore; I just didn't. I remember looking up and just being real honest with God. I said "If you show me that your real than I will show you a real Christian." And I walked out of that house. I asked my girlfriend to try again and it was awkward I promise you. But very quickly things began to change around me and not just around me but inside of me. I wanted to be different and do different,but still I didn't know how to and then I met a great person. Please understand that at the time I was tattooing out of my house. We met and she and I came up with a design and just like that I began to tattoo, but this time was different. As I tattooed her she would read the Bible and I remember her saying that it was because she was allergic to all pain medication and that reading the Bible was what helped the pain. We Tattooed for a pretty decent while and she would just talk to me and ask me questions. About half way through our session I asked her about something and I found out this woman had wealth. By the time we get done I find out that she wrote books about how she did it, so when it came time for payment I asked for a book instead. She leaves and comes back with multiple books, but not just that. She also gave me a curriculum for raising your children with a millionaire mindset and another curriculum for getting out of debt and to top it all off she even paid me for the tattoo and paid for me to go to a business seminar. She was an extremely sweet and generous person to me and I'm very thankful for her. May God remember the love she showed me and repay her for it. I was so excited to go to this seminar that I read one of her books all the way through. (It was the first real book I read all the way through)When I went to the first business meeting I met a couple there, that was also from Kerrville and we became friends. I made the choice to continue to go to these meetings and they began to take me to different places in America. My bond got even stronger towards these people that I had met at the meetings and we began to hangout outside of business classes. One day a woman that I had met at the first meeting and became friends with was having a Shabbat at her home. While we were all hanging out she began to talk about having this spiritual experience in a counseling session known as deliverance ministry. She ask me if I was into spiritual things and I responded yes so she asked me if I would be willing to meet with the person who does the counseling. I asked her what happened and she began to tell me a peculiar story about this man talking to her and a spirit or demon coming out of her. So I really wanted to know if what she told me was as real as she made it seem, so I got the number and while I was parked outside of Hastings in Kerrville and I made the call to set a day to meet with this man. The man answered and we made an appointment to meet at a place on water st..

Christians and demons I still remember the address it was on Water St. I walked in and I remember seeing this minister and immediately I heard a voice say

"Kill Him". Negative thoughts for me or at least what I thought with me thinking was not uncommon. I usually would brush them off and just ignore them, but what made this thought life-changing, was what happened when a Christian actively engaged in the spirit. He was walking in front of me drinking coffee and as I heard this voice speak, this man immediately turned and looked at me and said "Ignore that thought". And He said "That voice you heard that you think was a thought it wasn't your thought. Spirits talk to you by giving you their thoughts". Now when he said this I could see something right beside my face on my right side hovering near me. It was this gremlin looking thing about a foot tall and it started cursing at him and flipping him off. He asked me what it was doing, so I gave a vague description of what it was saying and doing, then he laughed and asked me to step into his office. After we sat down he asked me a very simple question " Where is your walk with God?". I spoke up and said "It was lost"; As much as I guess anybody's was. We spoke about some stuff and he led me in a prayer and to ask Jesus into my life. As I walked out of that building I know I paused And I knew I was different. I could feel something inside me that was so pure and clean that I called my girlfriend and told her I was gonna walk home and that I had a lot to think about.

You cannot serve two Gods Now when I got home I talked to my girlfriend about what happened and did my best to explain that I was now a Christian. So she asked me what do we do now. I told her that I didn't know but I knew I couldn't be around any bad stuff anymore. She very much did not appreciate getting rid of a bunch of stuff such as movies, objects, etc. Anything that could draw me back I wanted it out of the house. My second day as a Christian I laid down to go to bed and I got pulled into a demonic vision.

Demonic vision As I got pulled into this vision I remember it being very different from a dream. (Not lucid Dreaming) I was very conscious and aware and I found myself standing on the side of the road. It was very dark and there was a park across the street and before crossing the street I was waiting for this very sketchy person on a bike to pass by me. So as this person passed by me I was getting ready to walk when suddenly I heard a thing running up behind me, very fast and loud. And a hand reached around and grabbed my face, then he pulled me back towards him and stuck a knife in the side of my throat and tore it from one side to the other. The reason I say this was different from a dream is because I could feel all of it, all the physical pain and I could taste the iron in my blood and feel the warmth as it ran down the inside of my body. I was extremely terrified and I remember falling in the fetal position and wanting to die quick because of how horrible it was. Then he pulled out a gun and put it to my head and I remember thinking hurry up so I could die. He shot three times, but no bullets came out of the gun; only concussion waves. The vision shifted I got up and started running and I get to the park, but now everybody that's surrounding me and walking by me are covered in black clothing and have Daggers hanging off of all of them. I find myself standing Inside this park arena and these demons are brutal. They look at me and tell me that I am going to fight and I looked down and I am covered in daggers and standing in black. They spoke to me and said "This is your opponent". It was the demon or spirit that had just cut my throat. I didn't have enough time to talk because we were both thrown straight into combat. I remember swinging and just try not to get hit and he swung at me I ducked underneath him and as I turned I brought my elbow up and hit him right in his throat. He fell on the ground and started clawing at the ground because he couldn't breathe and I remember I was about to step on him and I felt someone speak softly. The Voice said "This is not who you are and you don't have to do this". And for a brief second I was about to stop, but then all the anger all the pain entered my body and I looked down at this person/spirit and I thought but not today. I began to step on him until I crushed in his head and I got thrown out of the vision and it was morning.

The heavenly vision I was about a year into my walk as a Christian and it was the month of January. The deliverance office had moved to a place on Sydney Baker and I had been seen the minister still. My life had already been bearing fruit of transformation of the Holy Spirit at work in my life, but something inside of me truly longed to know God so much more. It seemed to be an average day, I had actually Almost completed reading the New Testament; I was about 3/4 of the way through with it. Anyways, I walked into the deliverance office and I started a formal conversation with the minister about the fact that my dad was not going to be able to make his appointment. For me specifically I was pretty upset because I believed this was going to be my dad's breakthrough moment. So after that conversation with the minister he asked me how I was doing I believe and I started talking about this longing that I was having. That I wanted something to happen that couldn't be faked. Not to put down The charismatic side of American Christianity but I didn't want something to happen to me that could've been explained away. Him and another minister began to pray for me and as they did I remember a Christian sister walking in. Now this sister was someone that I believe I had heard about at the time, but didn't have a relationship with her or as far as I'm aware even a conversation with. As she entered the room I remember feeling a physical shift of sensation as though peace entered the room and everything else submitted. At the time I was pretty taken aback by that part and as she begin to pray I remember thinking that I was seeing some thing standing next to me which now I believe was a messenger (Angel). A couple seconds into the prayer

I remember a conversation starting between one minister and the others about some thing that she was seeing and asking if they saw it to. She walks up to the wall put her hand around it and comes back asking if I could see sparkles or gold dust On her hand. Then she asked me to go stand where she had just put her hand at, so I remember starting to walk that way and thinking to myself "Something is about to happen to me, but immediately after that I had a thought say "But nothing whatever happened to you". The second voice was very much wrong. As I stood there in my timberlands, only a fraction of a second past and what I believe to be The fire of God touched me. Actually, it was a lot more dramatic than that; it felt like I stepped on a bomb. As what felt like a mixture of fire, electricity, and power exploding through me I screamed. It was as though heaven itself invaded my body and I could feel a very different spiritual sense. I could feel not just my flesh but everything. After I screamed and became very terrified, Becky asked me "What do you feel?" and I couldn't really gather my words. I began to try to control my breathing at that moment because I was shaking pretty dramatically and I started hearing a specific melody type humming sound, but the sound seemed a very far off. As I focused on the sound immediately light over took everything. It enter the room from the right side and wrapped everything and I was thrown into the vision. The first thing I noticed was that I was there and that it was pretty vast.There were people standing not too far away from me; I believe looking at me. A person appeared in front of me and they looked kind of like a mixture of vapor and light. I couldn't make out who the person was at first, it was kind of like having a word on the tip of your tongue but with your eyes. I knew that I knew them and as I started looking at them, I found myself picking up spiritually on who they were like speaking heart to heart. And then it hit me this was my uncle my dad's oldest brother. As soon as I knew who he was, he vanished the same way he came in front of me like vapor light is the same way he left. After that this book immediately came up moving really fast towards me and opened up in front of me. I remember seeing different rows of names all of which were written in black except for one name on the right hand side towards the middle of the page; it was my name. One thing that made this experience very real to me is that I did not tell Justin or Becky about the book, but they started talking about seeing a book while all this was happening. As I'm looking at this book a small creature like thing about four inches tall jumped off of me and started scratching my name out in the book. I very calmly said "No" and it became like dark vapor and was removed. My name which was written in gold went straight back to normal where I could see it without the scratches and the book was closed. Now a lot of other stuff happened to me during this experience. Something like a second me was taken out with a rope of light and pulled down and away from me. I begin to feel fear and things were screaming inside of me telling me to run out of the building and I chose not to. At one point this angel pulled a sword out faster than my thoughts could even register and looking back at him I remember kind of saying "please don't" and he shot straight through me; sword first of course. I didn't feel any pain but I opened up my eyes and I saw like a purple vapor of smoke come out of my chest and go up the side of the wall and a flash of light following it until they had both exited the room. I saw beautiful walkways that look like marble gold with translucent light flowing through it and a very soft pink magenta smoke that kept falling in on itself at the edge of the sides of the road. I had a very beautiful experience there and I was honestly forever changed.

Boat or Ark… your choice.

Opening statements:

1) Before I get into this teaching I'm reminded of Peter when Jesus called him out of the boat to trust him and look to him for the impossible, as many of us today,that are going to be listening to this message are looking for the answer to our problems to our circumstances to those things in our families that seem to be damaged and unable to be repaired.

2) I wanna remind you that as we go through the historical accounts in the Old Testament and the New Testament we will find that God Often uses those that may not have what modern eyes look to as great resources or perhaps great advantages in the natural, but He uses very often those that have given up hoping on everything that they can do and cast themselves to the mercy of God for their breakthroughs in the darkest situations.

Points:

1) What do I mean by Boat and what do I mean by Ark?

* When I say boat I'm referring to everything that you can control and everything done in self will for the direction of your life.

* When I say Ark I'm referring to someone that has given up there right in there situation to will, dictate or to force A path into their breakthrough.

2) The reason I have chosen this teaching at this moment in time is because I believe that there is something coming; a storm. No doubt that 2020 to 2022 has been very difficult and I would say a storm for many people; I believe it is going to get worse for some.

And I want to give the option for you to put your trust in Jesus as your Ark for the storm. Many of you are going to face the temptation in the decision to control your path and to force others to agree with you so that you can derive some form of comfort, but I will say to you now and the presence of God don't do it. Don't trust in your strength or in the opinions that you can conjure up that might sound reasonable but in the end will leave you without hope and destroyed and possibly even take those in the boat of your decision with you to destruction.

* I'm referring to all those that are in-trusted to you; your friend groups if you're a parent then your children if your husband than I'm referring to your wife and your kids.

3) Where can I find this in scripture?

There are plenty of scriptures for this principle, but we will refer to four of the historical accounts in scripture. Noah, Moses, Jonah, and Peter. Two will be called physical Arks. One will be a metaphoric Ark with the same principle and for Peter a spiritual Ark with physical manifestations; that are byproducts of true faith in Christ.

Noah is called a preacher of righteousness and in his account it reads.

13 And God said to Noah, "I have determined to make an end of all flesh, for the earth is filled with

violence through them. Behold, I will destroy them with the earth. [14] Make yourself an ark of gopher wood. Make rooms in the ark, and cover it inside and out with pitch. -Gen. 6:13-14 (ESV)

This is a time when everybody was completely given over to evil and it says it every thought was evil continuously, But Noah he feared God and was a preacher of righteousness. There was a storm coming, but God's love for Noah gave him a warning and not only gave him a warning, but promised that he would save his household and even preserve the animals with a future generation.

(Is this your warning today?) Maybe you don't know God and maybe I'm just some kid that you're wondering why am I even reading this rather than ignoring him and moving on with my life, but maybe today's your warning and maybe today God is asking you to trust Him. And in trusting Him, not just save yourself but perhaps you're a little sister or a brother, mother or father.

In times of storms just like in Noah's day, that everything you needed to survive, all your provision all your entertainment and those that need to be with you. God prepares an Ark to house and provide for everything that is inside of it; only He knows how long the storm will last and how violent it will be for cleansing.

Now to Moses; who was Moses?

Moses was son of slaves and in his time of earths history there was a pharaoh that began to be afraid of the Israelites (The people of God) and pharaohs solution was killed the children; all the young boys and out of fear that the Israelites would rebel because if they're great number, he begins to send out his people to kill the young children in the land.Moses's mother saw that her child was beautiful and made the decision that she would hide her son and she did. She hid him for three months until she couldn't anymore. And she knew she couldn't control the situation anymore and she put her trust in God. How do I know?

How do I know that she put her trust in God? I know this because when you read the account of Exodus and its original language Hebrew. It reads

"3 When she could hide him no longer, she took for him a basket made of bulrushes and daubed it with bitumen and pitch. She put the child in it and placed it among the reeds by the riverbank." - Exodus 2:3 (ESV)

That word "basket" in the Hebrew is translated "Ark". She put her son in an Ark.

In times of distress all we can do is trust; no matter what anybody tells you; their knowledge it's foolishness it doesn't start with the fear of God. Proverbs 1 verse 7 states "The fear of the Lord is the beginning of knowledge, But fools despise wisdom and instruction."

Maybe you had someone in your life and it feels like they are going to die or that you've lost all hope in protecting them. Maybe it's a son or a daughter that has runaway or that is immersed in the world with all of its lust. And you don't know what to do anymore you've tried, you've cried and you've talk to people and ask for all sorts of advice, but you haven't trusted in God and giving them up to the Ark who is Jesus.

Now to Jonah, Jonah was a man that knew what God had already spoken and maybe there's someone here listening. That God his already said something and maybe you did exactly what Jonah did.

Jonah ran from God. Santanna's advice for the day; "Do not do that!"

Because just like Jonah God has a way of getting you back.

Because of God's love for you because you were made for such a time as this and because he made the works before he made you; he knows how to get you back. He knows you,He loves you and the love of the father disciplines the Son that He loves.

Please keep in mind though that when you rebel against God and what he has told you to do and you know better; you become a very dangerous person to those around you. I want to be clear and easy to understand when I say this; God throws a storm at Jonah and Jonah because he was running and because there were people around him that were on the boat trying to do everything in their own strength, they were caught in the storm. And while y'all listen to me I want y'all to understand also that God has a storm for everyone of you and although God may not always be the one throwing them; he will use them to get you back on track. So where does this principal about a boat in an Ark makes sense in this story, well it's not the end of the story. After these people give up all hope and are trying to figure out why is this happening what have we done and on whose account is this happening to us. Jonah comes clean and says I know why it's because I'm running from God. And they ask him what are we to do with you to calm the storm. Let me read to you the account.

"12 And he said to them, "take me and throw me into the sea; then the sea will becomes calm for you. For I know that this great tempest is because of me." Jonah 1:12 (ESV)

Now jumping to verse 17

"17 Now the LORD had prepared a great fish to swallow Jonah. And Jonah was in the belly of the fish three days and three nights." Jonah 1:17 (ESV)

I would like to say that it's your way on the boat or Gods Way in the fish. This is the principal of the ark where you give up your hope in the storm and give up trusting in your rebellion and finally your attitude changes. And it becomes OK God I'll do it … I'll do things your way! Let's not laugh at Jonah because I am convinced that God can have a fish for you too. A place where He draws you into himself, away from everybody and in your own wilderness and begins to deal with you and begins to transform you to the person fit for the job to what God has called you to.

Now Peter, oh Peter; the man that I think so many people can relate to. The man that tries to do everything to please God and yet the man that sinks. The one who is trying to help and yet sometimes speaks and says the wrong thing.

Some have been this man in this part of his life to some degree. I wanna talk about the possibility of a life that chooses not the boat, not to try to craft your own way and to rely on everything that you can control, but I want to talk about the possibility of choosing Christ the ark of your salvation. The only one who can give you rest and the only one that you can come to the father through. It's stated in the Holy Scriptures that no one can come to the father but through him.

Peter is on a boat with the rest of the disciples in Matthew 14 and it states.

25 And in the fourth watch of the night he came to
them, walking on the sea. 26 But when the disciples
saw him walking on the sea, they were terrified, and
said, "It is a ghost!" and they cried out in fear. 27 But
immediately Jesus spoke to them, saying, "Take heart;
it is I. Do not be afraid."

28 And Peter answered him, "Lord, if it is you,
command me to come to you on the water." 29 He
said, "Come." So Peter got out of the boat and walked
on the water and came to Jesus. 30 But when he saw
the wind, he was afraid, and beginning to sink
he cried out, "Lord, save me."31 Jesus immediately
reached out his hand and took hold of him, saying
to him, "O you of little faith, why did you doubt?"
32 And when they got into the boat, the wind ceased.
– Matt. 14:25-32 (ESV)

I wanna give y'all my insight and you decide if this is you. Peter sees the Lord and He says take courage don't be afraid and he began to trust and as he's going about his life trusting God and walking towards him suddenly there's some wind and as it picks up as your mom begins to get sick and as your marriage begins to fall apart as a storm begins to be seen we become afraid.

We take our eyes off Jesus and we begin to sink. Maybe just like Peter it's time to cry out "Lord save me!" Maybe it's time to cry Lord I'm sorry maybe it's time to cry out I can't deal with this anymore and just like in the story I trust that Jesus will mediately stretch out his hand and catch you.Faith is sometimes hard to do, faith means to trust and it means to believe and it means to have confidence. And sometimes in the storms it's hard to have confidence when you're not in control when you're not the one making the decisions. The one deciding which path to take and deciding when to let the sails down and when to fold them back up again. It says without faith it is impossible to please God and inside the ark faith is all you have. Faith that God will protect your family faith that God can break your drug addiction faith that God can help you get over pornography and to be sanctified and washed. Like Peter on the water, all things are possible with God.

I want to invite you to accept Jesus in Faith and trust him not just for the storm that is coming but for the rest of your life.

* New heart
* New mind
* New spirit
* New nature

"[17] Therefore, if anyone is in Christ, he is a new creation. The old has passed away; behold, the new has come." - 2 Corinthians 5:17 (ESV)

Study tools or mistresses I would like to start off by saying my concern is not that Christians have written about what God has shown them and want to get that experience into the hand of others, after all that is exactly what I'm doing. My main concern is that when all you do is recommend books for others to read, I believe that you in a way rob them of an opportunity to grow with God their Father. God says in Proverbs that it is his glory to conceal a matter and it is the glory of the king to search that matter out. I think it is an awesome thing when you can read a book about someone's experience And what took them 60 years to learn and figure out you can do that in a week reading their book. Please understand that I am not against that. But when you are a new Christian it is very important I believe, that you read God's word and you Ask, seek and knock; by yourself. It's important that you learn to depend on him for answers and information and not always google or run to a Christian book for that answer. It's an opportunity to grow a relationship of dependence and when all you do is read everybody else's interpretation you can very well miss out on the interpretation that God wanted to give you. When learning how to prophesy I had seen the very same thing. People would ask God for a word of encouragement and when they believed he gave them a picture or a certain phrase, instead of asking God what it meant they would Google it or ask someone else and hinder their relationship from going deeper with Him. Study tools are useful, but relationship is better.

My concern with Christians and money First I would like to say that I believe a lot of how American Christians treat their money has a lot to do with culture in America. We are presented with so many different ways in America for how a Christian should treat their money. Most honest millionaires that I have heard will tell you that the books they sell are useful tools but all the stuff they teach in principal about money were taken out of the Bible. I think Christians in America sometimes try to justify making money off of other believers by quoting scriptures. Whether it's "For the Scripture says, "You shall not muzzle an ox when it treads out the grain," and, "The laborer deserves his wages."- 1 Timothy 5:18 (ESV)

"And remain in the same house, eating and drinking what they provide, for the laborer deserves his wages. Do not go from house to house." -Luke 10:7 (ESV)

"Acquire no gold or silver or copper for **your belts,** [10] no bag for your journey, or two tunics[a] or sandals or a staff, for the laborer **deserves his food.**"- Matthew 10:9-10 (ESV)

These scriptures help me to understand that the believer will be taken care of because of what they do. It does not teach that you are entitled to take money from brothers and sisters and spend it on yourself until you think you have the materialistic life you believe God wants for you. When I first started a ministry, I told God something like "whatever comes in for ministry it's for you and it's not for me to spend on myself. If you want me to be wealthy give me strategy with the money that I make apart from ministry at my work. Help me to understand the difference". I understand to a degree that people are just trying to build up the kingdom in the way that they think it's supposed to be built up. But I also see times When 'christians' promote themselves or their new book from the platform that God gave them To teach his word. Now you may not think that's the case, but from somebody that spent thousands of dollars investing in learning about business, I know a business model when I see one. Revelation and understanding cannot be bought from God and it should not be sold by his children to other brothers and sisters. It seems that some Christians in America have forgotten that what God gave you was free and you are freely supposed to give it to those in need. I understand this is not a popular opinion and you may even be quoting scripture in your head trying to justify what you do as I am quoting scripture in different places to justify what I believe is true, but brother/sister listen to me when I say this next phrase. Store up for yourself treasures in heaven where thieves do not break in and steal and where moths don't devour. Jesus told the rich person to sell all that you have and give to the poor and you will have treasure in heaven. We all have a relationship to walk out, I'm not asking you to become homeless but I am asking you to use your freedom for the benefit of others. Once again I would just like to clarify I'm not against you having wealth, but how much money is too much? Answer: When you rely on the money for security and not God; you can only serve one.

MILK AND MEAT "11 About this we have much to say, and it is hard to explain, since you have become dull of hearing. 12 For though by this time you ought to be teachers, you need someone to teach you again the 'basic principles of the oracles of God'. **You need milk, not solid food**, 13 for 'everyone who **lives on**

milk is unskilled in the word of righteousness, since he is a child'. 14 But **solid food is for the 'mature'**, for those who have their 'powers of discernment trained' by 'constant practice' to distinguish good from evil."- Hebrews 5:11-14 (ESV)

"But I, brothers, could not address you **as spiritual people,** but of the as people flesh, as '**infants'** in Christ. 2 I fed you with **milk**, not **solid food**, for you were not ready for it. And even now you are not yet ready, 3 for you are still of the flesh. For while there is **jealousy and strife among you**, are you not **of the flesh** and behaving only in a human way? 4 For when one says, "I follow Paul," and another, "I follow Apollos," are you not being merely human?5 What then is Apollos? What is Paul? Servants through whom you believed, as the Lord assigned to each. 6 I panted, Apollos watered, but God gave growth."- 1 Cor. 3:1-5 (ESV)

NOTES: When reading the scripture above we can have a little insight about how church discipline is addressed among the disciples. In the last verse shown, verse 6 it is a mature answer to a child's argument. The less learned disciples seem to be falling into the snare that the apostles fell into when they followed Jesus, they may not be arguing over who is the greatest but in a sense which servant they are under is. Be sure to keep watch on what people are are focusing on or what fruit is visible in their walk with God. This shows a great understanding of what it is to be spiritual/mature! Paul is reminding them that God is the one who gives growth and is who we serve. You are not spiritual if you have jealousy and strife among you as seen above in 1 Cor. 3:3 (ESV) If you are getting milk and not solid food you are not yet mature, but considered to be people of the flesh, infants in Christ. However there are ways for each of us to train ourselves in Christ and in his word. The writer of Hebrews says "you need someone to teach you again the 'basic principles of the oracles of God.' – Hebrews 5:12 (ESV) Learning from this will show clearly that the person who is both skilled in the word of righteousness and who has had their powers of discernment trained by constant practice to distinguish good from evil is the mature.

Milk (unskilled)	Solid food (Mature)
Infants in Christ	Mature in Christ
Dull of hearing	Can hear
Still in the flesh	Is considered spiritual
Need someone to teach you again the basics principles of the oracles of God	Skilled in the word of righteousness
Needs their powers of discernment trained	Has their powers of discernment trained
Needs constant practice distinguishing good from evil	Does have constant practice distinguishing good from evil
Doesn't yet have hidden wisdom of God	Interpreting spiritual truths
Does not yet judge all things	Judges all things

Please take your time looking up at the chart and reflecting on how your personal walk with the Holy Spirit is going. Many of us have had our own fair share of growing and learning to be apart of this family known as the Body of Christ. I don't want you to fill discouraged, but I do want you to be honest with yourself. Honesty is a very good thing and a characteristic of a mature believer in Christ. In my younger days of growing as a Christian I learned that although being zealous for God could show boldness, it could also show my lack of understanding and or my lack of relationship with Gods word. I want to remind you that proverbs 4:5 (ESV) says "Get wisdom; get understanding; and do not forget, and do not turn away from the words of my mouth." Wisdom is a great asset that God gives to the son or daughter that ask of Him, but also consider getting understanding. The reason I bring this up is because in 1Peter 3:15-16 (ESV) we see that because of the lack of our understanding in scripture, that the untaught and unstable twist it for their own destruction. It is useful to study to show your self approved and to be growing in the pure spiritual milk towards the solid foods of scripture. The spirit of God will guide you so do not fear because when Jesus spoke he said “I will not leave you as orphans; I will come to you.” Be strong and do not give up. **More study scriptures**:” [6] Yet among the mature we do impart wisdom, although it is not a wisdom of this age or of the rulers of this age, who are doomed to pass away. [7] But we impart a secret and hidden wisdom of God, which God decreed before the ages for our glory. [8] None of the rulers of this age understood this, for if they had, they would not have crucified the Lord of glory. [9] But, as it is written,

> “What no eye has seen, nor ear heard,
> nor the heart of man imagined,
> what God has prepared for those who
> love him”- 1 Cor. 2:6-9 (ESV)

This is amazing we only impart to the mature a secret wisdom and hidden wisdom of God that God decreed before the ages for ‘our’ glory! “And we impart this in words not taught by human wisdom but taught by the Spirit, interpreting spiritual truths to those who are spiritual. [14] The natural person does not accept the things of the Spirit of God, for they are folly to him, and he is not able to understand them because they are spiritually discerned. [15] The spiritual person judges all things, but is himself to be judged by no one. [16] "For who has understood the mind of the Lord so as to instruct him?" But we have the mind of Christ."1 Cor. 2:13 (ESV)The mind of Christ is talked about in The book of Philippians "2 complete my joy by being of the same mind, having the same love, being in full accord and of one mind. 3 Do nothing from selfish ambition or conceit, but in humility count others more significant than yourselves. 4 Let each of you look not only to his own interests, but also to the interests of others. 5 Have this mind among yourselves, which is yours in Christ Jesus," –Phil. 2:2-5 (ESV) "**2** So put away all malice and all deceit and hypocrisy and envy and all slander. [2] Like newborn infants, long for the pure spiritual milk, that by it you may grow up into salvation— [3] if indeed you have tasted that the Lord is good. - 1 Peter 2:1-3 (ESV) " [15] And count the patience of our Lord as salvation, just as our beloved brother Paul also wrote to you according to the wisdom given him, [16] as he does in all his letters when he speaks in them of these matters. There are some things in them that are hard to understand, which the ignorant and unstable twist to their own destruction, as they do the other Scriptures."- 2 peter 3:15-16 (ESV)

Really taking the time to understand these things is going to help both you and your future disciples and those you are called to teach. It is a very important and a serious thing when you were called to lead in the body of Christ. Let this be your warning when you stand in judgment that you were warned. I am not trying to scare you, but I am trying to be very serious with you. It is written by the first century church that we will undergo a greater judgment because of those who we instructed. Do your best and keep the faith and abide in the love of God and may Christ be with you.

Exercise: Repent for all things that you have done wrong or for self-gain and self-promotion. Understand that you are loved and you can fully commit to growing in God and doing it his way.

Stable or blind [3] His divine power has granted to us all things that pertain to life and godliness, through the knowledge of him who called us to his own glory and excellence, [4] by which he has granted to us his precious and very great promises, so that through them you may become partakers of the divine nature, having escaped from the corruption that is in the world because of sinful desire. [5] For this very reason, make every effort to supplement your faith with virtue, and virtue with knowledge, [6] and knowledge with self-control, and self-control with steadfastness, and steadfastness with godliness, [7] and godliness with brotherly affection, and brotherly affection with love. [8] For if these qualities are yours and are increasing, they keep you from being ineffective or unfruitful in the knowledge of our Lord Jesus Christ. [9] For whoever lacks these qualities is so nearsighted that he is blind, having forgotten that he was cleansed from his former sins. [10] Therefore, brothers, be all the more diligent to confirm your calling and election, for if you practice these qualities you will never fall. [11] For in this way there will be richly provided for you an entrance into the eternal kingdom of our Lord and Savior Jesus Christ. – 2 Peter 1:3-11 (ESV). What I am hoping to do is to keep you on the right path as we study the Word together. Many of you may not seem like the ones that would have been chosen to learn about this or even to be chosen for the kingdom of Our Lord Jesus, but if you are here than it was God leading you to be. As we go through this we will learn much together and many of you may have encounters with the holy spirit; this is welcomed here. Please feel free to ask God as many questions as you would like . Do not think that having questions makes you dull or out of place. Its very important to seek and gain understanding from scripture whether for welfare, ministering, teaching etc. Each one of you carry unique qualities in your relationship with Jesus and have a place in the body. If you do not yet know where you belong in the body than I would urge you to ask for wisdom on this. God has promised that if we lack wisdom than to ask and it would be freely given. To start off this lesson we will be learning what each word means in context. Understanding context and the truth about what God says about us will help you grow into maturity and begin to help others more effectively.

Always simplify your study sheet

The Word	The meanings
Faith: What is faith defined as?	Original Word: πίστις, εως, ἡ Part of Speech: Noun, Feminine Transliteration: pistis Phonetic Spelling: (pis'-tis) Definition: faith, faithfulness Usage: faith, belief, trust, confidence; fidelity, faithfulness.
Virtue: What is virtue defined as?	Original Word: ἀρετή, ῆς, ἡ Part of Speech: Noun, Feminine Transliteration: areté Phonetic Spelling: (ar-et'-ay) Definition: moral goodness, virtue Usage: goodness, a gracious act, virtue, uprightness.
Knowledge: What is knowledge defined as?	Original Word: γνῶσις, εως, ἡ Part of Speech: Noun, Feminine Transliteration: gnósis Phonetic Spelling: (gno'-sis) Definition: a knowing, knowledge Usage: knowledge, doctrine, wisdom
Self-Control: What is self-control defined as?	Original Word: ἐγκράτεια, ας, ἡ Part of Speech: Noun, Feminine Transliteration: egkrateia Phonetic Spelling: (eng-krat'-i-ah) Definition: mastery, self-control Usage: self-mastery, self-restraint, self-control, continence

Steadfastness:
What is steadfastness defined as?

Original Word: ὑπομονή, ῆς, ἡ
Part of Speech: Noun, Feminine
Transliteration: hupomoné
Phonetic Spelling: (hoop-om-on-ay')
Definition: a remaining behind, a patient enduring
Usage: endurance, steadfastness, patient waiting for.

godliness:
What is godliness defined as?

Original Word: εὐσέβεια, ας, ἡ
Part of Speech: Noun, Feminine
Transliteration: eusebeia
Phonetic Spelling: (yoo-seb'-i-ah)
Definition: piety
Usage: piety (towards God), godliness, devotion, godliness.

Brotherly affection:
What is brotherly affection defined as?

Original Word: φιλαδελφία, ας, ἡ
Part of Speech: Noun, Feminine
Transliteration: philadelphia
Phonetic Spelling: (fil-ad-el-fee'-ah)
Definition: the love of brothers, brotherly love
Usage: brotherly love, love of Christian brethren.

Love:
What is Love defined as?

original Word: ἀγάπη, ης, ἡ
Part of Speech: Noun, Feminine
Transliteration: agapé
Phonetic Spelling: (ag-ah'-pay)
Definition: love, goodwill
Usage: love, benevolence, good will, esteem; plur: love-feasts.

The reason that I'm writing about this specific part of scripture right now is because Jesus told us that there is a Broadway that leads to destruction and a lot of people find it, but also there's a narrow way that leads to life and that it's difficult and few people find it. But even though it's difficult I love the fact that Peter gave us a form of instruction that if we practice, we will not only bear fruit but Peter says for if you practice these qualities you will never fall. For in this way there will be richly provided for you an entrance into the eternal kingdom of our Lord and Savior Jesus Christ. I believe he gave us these eight Qualities to practice to teach us how to stay on the right path and not get caught up in the enemies snares. I'm doing my very best to equip you in the way that I believe will be very beneficial for your relationship with the Holy Spirit, Jesus and God the Father. The way that I am attempting to teach you it's to give you a basic understanding of some specific scriptures and for you to search and take them deeper until God reveals to you something that is new for you.

We as Christians will be known by our fruit. It's very important that we bear it both in season

and out of season. It can be very difficult and by yourself it is impossible, but with God all things are possible. Don't take for granted The brothers and sisters that God has planted around you. Start to build relationships and hold one another accountable for your actions. A brother once told me that there is a difference between being transparent with somebody and being vulnerable with somebody. Being transparent has to do with what you had gone through in the past and being vulnerable is about talking about what you are presently going through. Choose to be vulnerable with one another. Love each other and hold each other accountable and if one falls lift them back up. You do have a choice to choose what will do for Gods glory, but I urge you to make your choice with wisdom and in prayer. Without repentance and mercy you will face the ramifications of your actions. I love you and please take this as a warning. (Keep the Faith and stay close to God).

God answered my prayer with responsibility Many people it seems like don't understand a real simple principle about the kingdom. And I didn't either, this principle is called stewardship. Sometimes when we pray we ask for things and because we don't understand stewardship we believe our prayer went unanswered. Here's a basic example:

You: God please give me a forest.
God: Here is one seed. ☺
You: God please give me a forest
God:.....
You: God don't you love me? Do you hear me?
God: 😒
You: It must not be your will sorry I even asked 😭😭😭😭
God:....
You: I love you; not my will but your will be done.
Holy Spirit: Excuse me (softly Spoken)
You: Yes?
Holy Spirit: What is inside of a Seed?
You: A plant 🌱
Holy Spirit: And when that plant drops 100 seeds; what will be inside of those seeds?
You: 😲😲 sudden epiphany 😲😲

Stewardship is very important because it helps develop your character. Developing your character is a very important thing. If you are put in charge of something and you do not have the character to sustain the position in which you have been put, then you will be put in a very bad Situation. I believe right now that is what is happening in America with this younger Generation. They don't understand the cost of freedom that was paid to get the nation to this point and because they never had to fight for it, they now don't have the character developed to sustain what they've been given so they are squandering the blessing. How you choose to Steward the seeds in your life and the answers you get in seed form will determine what you are put in charge of in the kingdom. In this example the person failed to see that the forest was in the seed.

The cycle of suffering or growth "[3] Not only that, but we rejoice in our sufferings, knowing that suffering produces endurance,[4] and endurance produces character, and character produces hope, [5] and hope does not put us to shame, because God's love has been poured into our hearts through the Holy Spirit who has been given to us."- Romans 5:3-5 (ESV)

I absolutely love this portion of scripture! So basically what I get from the scripture is that God actually has a reason for your suffering. Also remember I'm not saying that God is the one bringing about every suffering, but using it for your benefit. When you are going through suffering you begin to endure it and in that enduring you actually start to develop a character that produces hope; how amazing. But what happens when you in anguish interfere with the cycle? The way I see this taking place is as followed. You begin to suffer and in that suffering you begin to endure, but then because Of your lack of prayer and relationship you fall into temptation and begin to look for a way out of the endurance. Now instead of you getting the character that produces hope which comes from having to be patient in the endurance process, you begin to partner with different characters to ease the process of your suffering, maybe pornography maybe anger or maybe even bitterness and resentment. Because you did not have patience to endure and wait on God's character to be developed in you but partnered with another and you are now feeling hopeless. God loves you whether you like it or not and wants to make a change in your life for the better.

Trust him and trust his process because he will not let you down. In my short time as a Christian let me tell you what I have found out, God is faithful. Draw near to him and he will draw near to you. Also seek him with all your heart and he will be found by you and manifest himself to you. (If you truly want to walk with God you must trust him)

Do we just not know or are we choosing to be ignorant The more I read about or hear talks about how our Christian brothers and sisters have acted in history I feel that I am spiritually provoked to go deeper. Jesus is the same yesterday, today and forever. Although this is true, culture has not been the same yesterday, today nor will it be tomorrow. So why do we make the choice of choosing culture over Christ? One is the truth and it's everlasting and the other will perish and pay the price of not being able to be with him. Jesus himself told us that you either gather or you scatter, yet so many times we find ourselves compromising. Whether that's because of circumstances that cause fear, just because we are ignorant of who Christ is or what he says to us. It does not change the fact that we can be wrong and no amount of your justification will save you. You see in America we have a very dangerous privilege and that privilege is freedom. Freedom can be a very awesome and amazing thing when it is utilized the right way. And it can be a very dangerous thing when it is taken for granted and used as a crutch to not go deeper because of the lack of resistance. A lot of the reason that I believe we are taking our freedom for granted has to do with what I see coming our way. It seems to me that we will either make the conscious choice to trust and follow Christ As true believers or we will be forced into a situation where we have to trust him and then find out is your foundation rooted in truth. God will not be mocked and unless America receives mercy and forgiveness for the blood that was spilled and evils that were done in it, we will reap what has been done in it. We are called to pray and we are called to be lights that cannot be hidden. Yet we dim ourselves because of the lack of relationship and obedience to walk out what we were commanded to walk out. Jesus spoke clearly to us that whoever finds his life will lose it, and whoever loses his life for my sake will find it. God may ask many of us to stand up and to be his ambassadors and some of us may very well pay a high price for it. Are you truly convinced? As so many other brothers and sisters were convinced, that you will lose your life for His sake. What a hard question to ask. I'm honestly not sure how many of us would stand up and that possibly has something to do with what the word Christian means in America; it's been diluted. And in other places of the world it holds true to it's biblical meaning. I am a Christian, I follow Christ, and I will say what God says. What God says is good is good and what God says his evil is evil and we don't try to change it. It doesn't matter the circumstance and as hard as that may be it is better to suffer a little while and be with him, than not suffer now and lose relationship with him forever. We have access to so many things in America and we have the freedom for as long as God chooses for us to have it to speak out and to love those who are lost. What are we doing with our time? Are we taking the time to pray for those that have hurt us and for those that are lost? Are we studying to show ourselves approved? Are we being conformed to the image of Christ? Do you even want those that everyone else says are too far gone to be granted mercy? We must become real

Christian and give up a lukewarm lifestyle centered in cultural beliefs.

My final plea to you Do your very best and endure every trial that comes your way. If you're a husband love your wife and remember that you will be held accountable for everything you do and if you miss treat your wife that your prayers will actually be hindered.(1 Peter 3:7 (ESV)) Your contribution to the body of Christ can make a difference; it really can. Gods word tells me that a teacher will receive a greater judgment,but I am still trying to make a difference by teaching you what I've learned. Think about that, I don't know where you are in your maturity And I don't know if you will misinterpret something. Everything that you have read please compare it to scripture and search it out for yourself because that is the glory of a king. If you don't know Christ or if you say you do but don't walk in obedience to scripture then I'm speaking to you. God offers you a new life through his son Jesus and by excepting him as your savior, he offers you salvation. There is no other way or name by which you can be saved. If you want a new life and to be a new creature, then you must except the sacrifice that God gives. Scripture tells us that if you confess with your mouth and believe in your heart, than you will be saved. I love you and I've done my best to help you. I'm not saying it's gonna be easy, but I am saying that there will be somebody standing beside you that is closer than a friend. May God bless you and keep you and change your life forever. Love, your brother.

Printed in the United States
by Baker & Taylor Publisher Services